Gourmet
SAFARI

A gastronomic journey through the wonders of Africa

To my dearest love, Suku. Without your support and the occasional nudge, I would not be where I am today.

This book is also dedicated to the hardworking staff who make the 'magic' happen in all the camps. On behalf of the managers and operations staff, who could not do what they do without you, THANK YOU!

Sanctuary Baines' Camp, Okavango Delta, Botswana

Gourmet
SAFARI

A gastronomic journey through the wonders of Africa

DONOVAN VAN STADEN

CONTENTS

Introduction

A lot has changed in the safari world over the past few years. There are many more lodges and therefore the competition is fiercer than ever. However, this is a good thing because everyone has to raise their game to stay ahead of the pack. The standard of the cuisine is no exception from this pursuit of excellence. In fact, the bragging rights for having the best food in the industry is at the top of our list of goals. What this evolution has resulted in is a new generation of 'bush fine dining'. This is not always easy to accomplish when the supply truck is stuck somewhere between here and Malawi or on a boat somewhere in the Okavango Delta. That being said, no one said it was going to be easy, and we wouldn't want it any other way.

How would we describe our food? I'd say 'gourmet home cooking'. Take some good quality ingredients, add a dollop of respect and combine with a few good techniques. Blend until smooth, glossy and delicious and serve with a warm, welcoming smile.

It sounds simple enough, but this is only possible with the dedication of talented and hardworking teams. The true stars of the show are the chefs. Day after day they work tirelessly to produce the meals that keep our guests' bellies full and content. Without them none of this would be possible (including this book).

All recipes are by Donovan van Staden unless otherwise indicated.

About Sanctuary Retreats

Sanctuary Retreats was born in Africa with the launch of its first luxury safari camp, Sanctuary Olonana, in Kenya in 1999. We now own and operate an additional 13 lodges and camps in Zambia, Botswana, Tanzania and Uganda. We also offer private luxury camping across East Africa. Building on our heritage of luxury adventure travel, we also manage and run seven spectacular expedition cruise ships in some of the most remarkable cultural and ecological sites in the world. Five of our cruises explore epic rivers – including the Yangtze in China and the Nile in Egypt – while our other two ships journey through the awe-inspiring volcanic archipelago that is the Galápagos Islands. And the latest addition to our fleet is a beauty, setting sail in the wondrous land of Myanmar.

Website: www.sanctuaryretreats.com

KNOCK, KNOCK!

There's a 'knock, knock' just outside your tent and a steaming cup of coffee to help kick-start your engine. And don't forget the biscuits – the perfect accompaniment to that first cup of perfectly brewed dark roast. The day starts early in the bush, but trust me, it's worth it.

There is something incredible about waking up with the sun rising over your toes; only a thin layer of canvas between you and the wild African bush. Every sound is so clear – the rustle of a hippo heading past your tent on its way back to the river, or the breaking of branches as the elephants feed just outside your room.

This is Africa, and a glorious day is just beginning.

Vanilla Biscuits

Makes 20

250 g cake flour
120 g custard powder
120 g icing sugar
250 g butter
5 ml vanilla essence

Preheat the oven to 180 °C. Grease a baking tray and sprinkle some flour over the tray. Give the tray a good shake to spread the flour until the tray is thinly coated. Discard the excess flour. Mix all the ingredients together to form a smooth dough. Knead for 3–5 minutes and then set aside to rest for 15 minutes. Roll small balls of dough in the palms of your hands. The size of the ball will determine the size of the biscuit, but about half the size of a golf ball is a good start. Place the doughballs on the prepared tray, spaced about 5 cm apart. Using the tines of a fork, press the doughball down about halfway. Bake for 8–10 minutes. Allow to cool on the baking tray before placing in an airtight container. Enjoy with your favourite morning brew.

Ginger Biscuits
Makes 15

1 egg, beaten
110 g butter, melted
225 g self-raising flour
2.5 ml baking powder
225 g sugar
5 ml ground ginger
5 ml golden syrup

Preheat the oven to 180 °C. Grease a baking tray. Mix the egg and melted butter in a mixing bowl. Add the rest of the ingredients to the egg mixture and mix well until it forms a dough. Roll pieces of dough into small balls about half the size of a golf ball. Place on the prepared baking tray. Allow enough space for each ball to spread to form a biscuit shape. Bake for 15−20 minutes, or until golden brown. Cool on a wire rack and then store in an airtight container.

BREAKFAST

Sanctuary Olonana Safari Camp: Beautiful breakfast stop overlooking the vast plains of the Masai Mara National Park, Kenya

You are surprisingly hungry for this time of the morning and breakfast awaits. While I may enjoy a bowl of home-made muesli and Greek yoghurt to start the day, that doesn't mean the chefs aren't going to give you the royal treatment as far as a scrumptious breakfast is concerned. Tucking into a cheesy omelette before a morning drive may be exactly what the doctor recommends after a few too many campfire 'bush tales' the night before.

With everyone looking remarkably sprightly this early in the morning, you sit down to a delicious breakfast before heading out on the morning drive.

Apple and Cinnamon Muffins
Makes 12

250 g cake flour
190 g sugar
10 ml baking powder
5 ml ground cinnamon
2.5 ml bicarbonate of soda
pinch of salt
5 ml nutmeg
190 ml milk
2 eggs, beaten
75 g butter, melted
2 medium apples, chopped
120 g walnuts, chopped

Preheat the oven to 180 °C. Grease and flour a 12-cup muffin pan. In a large bowl, combine the flour, sugar, baking powder, cinnamon, bicarbonate of soda, salt and nutmeg. In a separate small bowl, beat the milk, eggs and melted butter until well blended. Stir the milk mixture into the flour mixture until just blended. Fold in the apples and walnuts. Spoon the batter into the prepared muffin cups, filling each three-quarters full. Bake for 25–30 minutes, or until a toothpick inserted in the centre comes out clean. Cool in the pan for 2 minutes. Turn out onto a wire rack to cool completely before storing them in an airtight container.

By Chef Morgan – Sanctuary Puku Ridge Camp, South Luangwa, Zambia

Apricot Puffs

Makes 9

250 g Basic Danish Pastry (see page 183)
2 large eggs, beaten
30 ml milk
120 g almond paste (marzipan)
9 tinned apricot halves, syrup drained
30 ml apricot jam, melted over medium heat

LEMON ICING
125 g icing sugar
15 ml freshly squeezed lemon juice
10 ml lemon zest
15 ml milk

Preheat the oven to 200 °C. Roll out the pastry into a 40 cm square. Cut the pastry into 18 equal-sized rounds. Place nine pastry rounds on a well-greased baking tray. Mix the eggs and milk together and brush the pastry with the egg wash. Place a teaspoonful of marzipan in the centre of each pastry round. Cut out a circle from the remaining nine rounds of pastry, about the size of the apricot halves. Place the pastry rounds on top of the marzipan and then insert an apricot half into the cut-out section, flat side facing up. Brush again with the egg wash. Bake on the top shelf of the oven until the pastry is crisp and golden. Remove the pastries from the oven and brush with the apricot jam.

For the lemon icing, combine all the ingredients. Allow the pastries to cool slightly before brushing them with the lemon icing.

By Chef Harry — Sanctuary Chief's Camp, Okavango Delta, Botswana

Cinnamon Flapjacks with Honey

Makes 10–12

250 g cake flour
110 g castor sugar
10 ml baking powder
5 ml ground cinnamon
90 g raisins (optional)
60 g butter, melted
375 ml milk
2 eggs
honey for serving

Mix the flour, castor sugar, baking powder, cinnamon and raisins together in a large jug or bowl. Mix the melted butter with the milk and eggs until well combined. Pour the milk mixture into the dry ingredients and mix well to a smooth batter consistency. Heat a nonstick frying pan and spoon one dollop of the flapjack batter into the pan. When the flapjack is a light brown colour underneath, turn it over and brown the other side. Remove from the pan and keep warm. Repeat until all the batter is used. Serve hot, drizzled with honey.

By Chef Ackim – Sanctuary Puku Ridge Camp, South Luangwa, Zambia

Cheese and Herb Scones
Makes 12–15

250 g cake flour
10 ml baking powder
175 g butter
30 ml roughly chopped parsley
1 small carrot, grated
100 g Cheddar cheese, grated
15 ml chopped red onion
pinch each of salt and ground black pepper
250 ml milk

Preheat the oven to 180 °C. Grease a baking tray. Mix the flour, baking powder, butter, parsley, carrot, cheese, onion, salt and pepper in an electric mixer until the mixture resembles bread-crumbs. Gradually add the milk until the mixture comes together and forms a dough. Knead for a few minutes until smooth. Roll out on a lightly floured surface to a thickness of 2 cm. Use a round cookie cutter (about 5 cm in diameter) to cut out the scones and place on the prepared baking tray. Brush milk over the top of each scone and bake for 30–45 minutes. Cool on a wire rack before storing in an airtight container.

Homemade Muesli
Makes about 1.3 kg

500 g oats
50 g cashew nuts
50 g almonds
50 g pecan nuts
30 g sunflower seeds
5 ml ground cinnamon
350 g sugar
125 ml sunflower oil
250 ml honey
150 g raisins
150 g sultanas

Preheat the oven to 160 °C. Mix the oats, nuts, sunflower seeds, cinnamon and sugar in a mixing bowl. Heat the oil and honey together in a saucepan. When hot, pour into the dry ingredients and mix well. Transfer the mixture to a large baking tray and spread out evenly. Bake for about 30 minutes. Stir halfway through the baking time to make sure the mixture doesn't burn. Bake until golden brown. Remove from the oven and mix in the raisins and sultanas. Cool completely and store in an airtight container.

Melon Balls in Champagne Syrup
Serves 8

150 g watermelon
150 g cantaloupe melon
150 g honeydew melon
sprigs of fresh mint for garnishing

CHAMPAGNE SYRUP
750 ml Champagne or sparkling wine
500 g sugar
1 cinnamon stick (6-cm piece)
2 star anise
2 vanilla pods, split lengthways (5ml vanilla essence)

Using a melon baller, scoop the watermelon, cantaloupe
and honeydew melon flesh into balls. Set aside.

For the Champagne syrup, place the Champagne, sugar,
cinnamon, star anise, and vanilla pods in a saucepan and bring
to a simmer. Reduce the liquid mixture by one-third.
Remove from the heat and allow to cool completely. Strain
the syrup into a plastic container, add the melon balls and
refrigerate overnight to allow the melon to fully absorb the
flavours of the syrup.

To serve, scoop chilled portions of melon into a glass, top
up with the syrup and garnish with a sprig of mint.

Eggs Benedict

Serves 4

HOLLANDAISE SAUCE
10 ml freshly squeezed lemon juice
10 ml white wine vinegar
3 egg yolks

POACHED EGGS
15 ml white wine vinegar
4 eggs
2 muffins, halved crossways
4 rashers streaky bacon, fried
sprigs of fresh parsley for garnishing (optional)
pinch each of salt and ground black pepper

For the Hollandaise sauce, whisk the lemon juice, vinegar and egg yolks in a small heatproof bowl until light and frothy. Place the bowl over a saucepan of simmering water and whisk until the mixture starts to thicken. If the mixture splits, add 5 ml water at a time and continue whisking.

For the poached eggs, add the vinegar to a small saucepan of water and bring to a simmer. (The vinegar helps the egg to bind.) Crack an egg into a cup. Stir the water to form a whirlpool and carefully tip the egg into the centre of the whirlpool. (NB: For the best results, use very fresh eggs otherwise they might not hold together in the water.) Poach the eggs one at a time until cooked to your liking.

To plate up, place half a muffin in the centre of the plate and top with the bacon and a poached egg. Spoon over the sauce. Garnish with a few sprigs of fresh parsley and season to taste.

By Chef Roy – Sanctuary Chichele Presidential Lodge, South Luangwa National Park, Zambia

On a game drive with Sanctuary Olonana Safari Camp , Masai Mara National Park, Kenya

MORNING DRIVE

Lion sighting at Sanctuary Stanley's Camp,
Okavango Delta, Botswana

Not a bad start to the day, with a long list of wild creatures already ticked off on your checklist.

It's about nine in the morning and that rumble in your stomach tells you that it's time for a morning coffee break. As if the intuitive guide heard the rumble too, he pulls up at the edge of a spectacular water hole dotted with hippos and the most colourful birds you have ever seen.

That cup of coffee and freshly baked treat hits the spot while you contemplate what you've already seen in the past few hours: two young giraffe bulls play-fighting; a grumpy elephant showing you who is boss; and let's not forget the majestic leopard basking in the golden morning light.

Muesli Bars
Makes 10–15

360 g rolled oats
70 g sesame seeds
140 g sunflower seeds
160 g desiccated coconut
140 g pumpkin seeds
150 g raisins
150 g sultanas
200 g butter
250 ml honey
50 g brown sugar

Grease a large baking tray and line it with greaseproof paper. In a heavy-bottomed frying pan, lightly toast the oats, sesame seeds, sunflower seeds, coconut, and pumpkin seeds. Allow to cool. Add the raisins and sultanas to the seed mixture. Place the butter, honey and sugar in a saucepan over medium heat until the sugar is completely dissolved. Bring to a simmer and reduce the syrup for 7 minutes. Pour the syrup into the seed mixture and combine well. Pour the mixture into the prepared baking tray and use the back of a large spoon to flatten and compress the mixture into an even layer. Allow to cool completely. Cut into bars or squares and store in an airtight container for up to one week.

'Walkaccino'

This is a speciality coffee served at our walking camp in South Luangwa, Zambia. Picture your-self out on a walking safari, sneaking your way around herds of elephant and grazing buffalo. And as if that isn't exciting enough, the guide then walks you up to a pride of sleeping lions. I will argue that there is no more exhilarating way to spend your morning.

'Right!' your guide exclaims, 'Anyone for a cappuccino?'

What? Here in the bush? And to your amazement the tea-bearer pulls an Italian stovetop per-colator and a milk frother out of his bag of tricks. Well, that would be useful if we had heat, you think to yourself. And then, as if the tea-bearer has read your mind, he pulls out his fire-making toolkit: a stick and a piece of wood.

Within 2 minutes there's a fire and then a few minutes later you're sipping on a delicious cappuc-cino in the middle of the African bush.

Sanctuary Puku Ridge Camp: A surprise river lunch in South Luangwa National Park, Zambia

LUNCH

*Santuary Swala Camp, Tarangire
National Park, Tanzania*

As you get back from the morning drive there is a much-needed fragrant face cloth and a cold drink waiting for you at the bar. The lunch menu is strategically placed next to your drink to whet your appetite. It is a small menu, with just enough options and variety to keep everyone's taste buds satisfied.

Sometimes words can't quite do justice to the wonders we encounter on a safari, such as enjoying lunch in the shade of a tamarind tree overlooking a flood plain teeming with wildlife. Just as your main course is served, a breeding herd of elephants makes its way to the water hole just in front of camp. The timing is perfect. As good as the food is, it cannot compete with this show, and everyone is mesmerised by the gentle beasts as they quench their thirst only a few metres away. As quickly as they arrived, the elephants quietly move off again, as if not wishing to disturb the tranquillity of the afternoon.

After lunch it is time for a well-deserved siesta. That delicious lunch has made your eyelids heavy, or was it that extra glass of Chardonnay? Whatever it was, it is time to tuck into that book you have been dying to read, and the daybed on your balcony looks like the perfect spot for the occasion.

Apple and Blue Cheese Salad
with Onion Marmalade
Serves 5

APPLE AND BLUE CHEESE SALAD
5 whole apples, peeled and cored
225 g cream cheese
80 g blue cheese
100 ml fresh cream
Onion Marmalade (see page 180) (optional)

DRESSING
125 ml olive oil
30 ml lemon juice
salt and ground black pepper to taste

For the salad, slice the apples across into five equally thick slices. Mix the cream cheese, blue cheese and cream together in a mixing bowl.

For the dressing, place the olive oil, lemon juice and seasoning in a screwtop jar. Shake vigorously until well combined.

To plate up, sandwich the apple slices together with the cheese mixture and position in the centre of each plate. Drizzle the dressing over and serve with the onion marmalade, if using.

Butternut Frittata with Stuffed Peppadews®

Serves 8

150 g butternut, peeled and chopped into 1 cm cubes
50 g potato, peeled and chopped into 1 cm cubes
30 ml sunflower oil
¼ onion, chopped
½ green pepper, chopped
½ red pepper, chopped
2 large spinach leaves, chopped
25 g feta cheese, crumbled
2 eggs
24 Peppadews®
250 g cream cheese
salt and ground black pepper

Preheat the oven to 180 °C. Boil the butternut and potato until soft. Set aside. Heat the oil in a large pan and fry the onion and peppers together until soft, and then add the spinach. After the spinach has wilted, add the cooked butternut and potato, as well as the feta cheese. Beat the eggs and add to the same mixture. Divide the mixture evenly between individual greased ramekins or dariole moulds, filling them three-quarters full to allow space for the frittatas to rise. Bake for 35 minutes. Remove from the oven and allow to cool. Stuff the Peppadews® with the cream cheese. Unmould the frittatas and serve with a fresh green salad and the stuffed Peppadews®. Season to taste.

By Chef Morgan – Sanctuary Puku Ridge Camp, South Luangwa, Zambia

Westphalia Ham and Melon Salad
with a Balsamic Reduction

This is my take on the traditional Italian Parma ham and melon duo.
Serves 1

BALSAMIC REDUCTION (MAKES 200 ML)
750 ml balsamic vinegar
250 g white sugar

HAM AND MELON SALAD
3 slices green melon
6 slices excellent quality Westphalia ham
salad greens

For the balsamic reduction, pour the vinegar into a saucepan and bring to a simmer. Add the sugar and reduce the liquid until it reaches a syrup consistency.
Chef's tip: Keep a very close eye on the balsamic mixture while it is reducing. It can go from simmer to burnt in the blink of an eye.

For the salad, wrap each piece of melon in a slice of ham. Place three slices of ham in the centre of the plate and arrange a small bundle of greens on top. Neatly stack the ham-wrapped melon on top of the greens. Drizzle the balsamic reduction around the salad.
Chef's tip: Try to get some height when plating up as it adds to the presentation.

Sanctuary Chichele Presidential Lodge: A walking safari in
South Luangwa National Park, Zambia

Meatball Soup

Serves 6

MEATBALLS
300 g beef mince
1 clove garlic, chopped
1 onion, chopped
50 g fresh breadcrumbs
1 egg
15 ml honey
pinch each of salt and ground black pepper

SOUP
15 ml olive oil
2 onions, chopped
3 cloves garlic, chopped
10 medium tomatoes, chopped
750 ml vegetable stock
2 red chillies, chopped
30 ml tomato paste
250 g pasta screws (fusilli)
20 fresh basil leaves

For the meatballs, mix all the ingredients together, then shape into small balls. Place in the freezer for 30 minutes. Preheat the oven to 220 °C. Coat the meatballs in oil and place on a baking tray. Roast for 15–20 minutes. Remove from the oven and set aside.

For the soup, heat the olive oil in a saucepan and sauté the onions and garlic until soft. Add the tomatoes, stock, chillies and tomato paste and boil for 15 minutes. Pour the soup into a blender and blend until smooth. Return the soup to the saucepan, bring back to a boil, add the meatballs and simmer for 15 minutes. Cook the pasta in salted boiling water until *al dente*. Stir the cooked pasta into the soup. Add the basil just before serving.

Green Pea Soup

A lovely summer soup for a lazy Sunday afternoon. It is best enjoyed chilled with a crunchy slice of Parmesan bruschetta.

Serves 6

45 ml sunflower oil
1 onion, chopped
4 cloves garlic, finely chopped
45 ml finely chopped fresh ginger
1 ml ground cumin
2 bay leaves
1 litre chicken or vegetable stock
500 g fresh peas (you can also use frozen peas)
salt and ground black pepper

Heat the oil in a large saucepan over medium heat. Add the onion, garlic and ginger and allow to soften. Add the cumin and bay leaves and sauté for 1 minute. Add the stock and bring to a simmer. Add the peas and bring back to a simmer for a few minutes. Don't simmer for too long otherwise the peas will lose their colour. Remove the bay leaves (and a few peas for garnishing) and purée the soup in a blender until smooth. If the soup is too thick, you can add more stock. Season to taste and refrigerate until well chilled.

Lamb Koftas with a Sweetcorn Salad and Cucumber Raita

Serves 6

LAMB KOFTAS
750 g lamb mince
1 onion, chopped
salt and ground black pepper to taste
5 ml ground cinnamon
18 kebab skewers
45 ml sunflower oil

SWEETCORN SALAD
1 onion, chopped
½ red pepper, chopped
½ green pepper, chopped
2 cloves garlic, chopped
45 ml chopped fresh basil
80 ml olive oil
15 ml lime juice
15 ml white vinegar
salt and ground black pepper to taste
350 g fresh corn kernels
2 tomatoes, seeded and chopped

CUCUMBER RAITA
see page 181

For the koftas, mix the mince with the onion, seasoning and cinnamon until well combined. Press the meat mixture onto the skewers in a sausage shape. To cook them you have two options: either shallow-fry the koftas in a frying pan, turning frequently until browned and cooked through, or bake them in the oven at 180 °C.

For the salad, place the onion, peppers, garlic, basil, oil, lime juice, vinegar and seasoning in a screwtop jar. Tighten the lid and shake vigorously until well combined. Combine the corn and tomatoes with the dressing and set aside for 20 minutes before serving with the koftas and cucumber raita.

Game Terrine with Homemade Chutney and Preserved Oranges

Serves 8

TERRINE
225 g pork sausage
225 g lean strips of kudu fillet (or you can use chicken)
1½ onions, finely chopped
1 clove garlic, finely chopped
2.5 ml ground allspice
40 ml good red wine
20 ml brandy
pinch each of salt and ground black pepper
2 eggs
250 g streaky bacon

PRESERVED ORANGES
see page 180

HOMEMADE CHUTNEY
see page 181

For the terrine, preheat the oven to 160 °C. Squeeze the pork mince out of the sausages and place in a mixing bowl with the kudu fillet strips. Add the onions, garlic, allspice, wine, brandy, salt, pepper and eggs. Mix well. Line a 1-litre terrine with the rashers of bacon, allowing them to overlap the rim of the terrine. Make sure there are no gaps. Fill the terrine with the meat mixture. Fold over the overhanging bacon to cover the top of the terrine. (If the rashers aren't long enough, place more rashers of bacon on top to cover the terrine mixture.) Place the terrine in a roasting pan half-filled with water (called a *bain-marie*). Bake in the oven for 1½–2 hours. The terrine is cooked when it shrinks away from the sides and a test skewer comes out of the centre piping hot and clean. Cool the terrine in the mould and keep in the fridge for a couple of days to allow the flavours to mature.

Serve thick slices of terrine with the preserved oranges and a good dollop of the chutney.

By Chef Lloyd – Sanctuary Chichele Presidential Lodge, South Luangwa National Park, Zambia

Honey-glazed Chicken Breast served with Vichy Carrots and Salsa

Serves 4

HONEY-GLAZED CHICKEN
125 ml soy sauce
30 ml sunflower oil
30 ml honey
1 clove garlic, chopped
5 ml finely grated fresh ginger
4 chicken breast fillets
5 ml cornflour
flat-leaf parsley for garnishing

VICHY CARROTS
10 medium carrots, peeled
30 ml sugar
500 ml water
50 g butter

SALSA
1 small avocado, peeled and chopped (optional)
1 tomato, seeded and chopped
1 onion, chopped
5 ml lemon juice

For the chicken, mix the soy sauce, oil, honey, garlic and ginger together to make a marinade. Marinate the chicken breast fillets for at least 1 hour, but preferably overnight. Preheat the oven to 180 °C. Remove the chicken from the marinade (reserve the marinade to make the sauce) and pan-sear the chicken breast fillets in a sizzling-hot frying pan. Once the chicken has been sealed and has some colour, transfer it to a baking tray and place in the oven for 15 minutes until just cooked through.

For the Vichy carrots, slice them into neat rectangles, all similar in size and shape. Place the sugar, water and butter in a saucepan and bring to a simmer. Add the carrots and simmer until they are just soft.

For the salsa, combine all the ingredients in a mixing bowl, cover and set aside.

For the sauce, place the reserved marinade in a saucepan, add the cornflour and whisk well. Bring the sauce to a boil and reduce until it reaches the required consistency.

To plate up, place some of the carrots in the centre of each plate, one overlapping the other to make a square. Place a chicken breast fillet on top of the carrots. Spoon about 15 ml salsa on top of the chicken and garnish with fresh flat-leaf parsley. Drizzle the sauce around the plate and serve immediately.

Warm Pork and Orange Salad
with a Mustard Dressing
Serves 4

MARINADE

45 ml sunflower oil

60 ml orange juice

15 ml wholegrain mustard

1 clove garlic, finely chopped

PORK AND ORANGE SALAD

1 kg pork fillet, trimmed

250 g green beans

1 head frilly lettuce

2 oranges, peeled and sliced crossways, 3–5 mm thick

1 large carrot, grated

fresh basil leaves for garnishing

MUSTARD DRESSING

90 ml mayonnaise

60 ml wholegrain mustard

1 clove garlic, crushed and chopped

30 ml orange juice

10 ml orange zest

For the marinade, mix all the ingredients together in a shallow dish. Place the pork fillet in the marinade and refrigerate for 1 hour.

For the salad, preheat the oven to 200 °C. Remove the pork fillet from the marinade and seal in a hot frying pan. Transfer the fillet to a roasting pan and roast in the oven for about 40 minutes, or until just cooked through. Set aside to cool slightly before cutting into slices. Poach the green beans until *al dente*.

For the dressing, mix all the ingredients until well combined.

To plate up, arrange a bed of lettuce in the centre of each plate. Layer the green beans on top of the lettuce and then arrange the pork fillet and orange slices neatly on top of the green beans. Sprinkle the grated carrot around the pork fillet and drizzle the dressing over the pork. Garnish with fresh basil.

Tilapia Croquettes with a Carrot and Bean Relish
Serves 6

CROQUETTES
5 ml paprika
pinch each of salt and ground black pepper
500 g tilapia or bream, filleted (deboned)
300 g potatoes, peeled
3 eggs, hard boiled and chopped
10 ml chopped fresh parsley
250 ml sunflower oil for deep-frying

BREADCRUMB COATING
60 g flour
3 eggs, beaten and seasoned
50 g dried breadcrumbs

CARROT AND BEAN RELISH
60 ml sunflower oil
2 onions, chopped
4 cloves garlic, chopped
30 ml grated fresh ginger
1 red chilli, chopped
30 ml curry powder
1 x 400 g tin whole peeled tomatoes, chopped
1 x 400 g tin butter beans
2 carrots, chopped
2 red peppers, seeded and chopped
2 green peppers, seeded and chopped
handful of fresh coriander, chopped

For the croquettes, prepare a saucepan of simmering water and add the paprika, salt and pepper. Poach the fish for 20–30 minutes, or until cooked. Remove the fish and flake the flesh, making sure there are no bones. Boil the potatoes in a separate saucepan until cooked through. Mash the potatoes with the fish and eggs. Add the parsley and salt and pepper to taste. Using your hands, mould the mixture into egg-shaped croquettes. Make three per portion.

For the breadcrumb coating, dust the croquettes in the flour, then dip into the beaten eggs and then the breadcrumbs. They should be completely coated in breadcrumbs. Set aside to dry for a few minutes. Heat the sunflower oil in a small saucepan deep enough for deep-frying. Deep-fry the croquettes until they are an even golden brown colour. Remove with a slotted spoon and set aside on paper towels to drain the excess oil.

For the relish, heat the oil and sauté the onions, garlic, ginger and chilli until the onions are soft. Add the curry powder and cook for a couple of minutes. Add the tomatoes and simmer for 10 minutes. Add the rest of the ingredients, except the coriander, and simmer for 15 minutes. Remove from the heat and add the coriander. Season to taste. Serve with the tilapia croquettes.

Hot Thai Beef Salad
Serves 6

MARINADE
2.5 ml chilli paste
15 ml sesame oil
3 cloves garlic, crushed
60 ml sweet soy sauce
5 ml finely grated fresh ginger
60 ml oyster sauce

SALAD
1 kg beef fillet, cut into strips
2 carrots, cut into strips
1 red pepper, cut into strips
1 yellow pepper, cut into strips
1 green pepper, cut into strips
200 g egg noodles, cooked
spigs of fresh parsley for garnishing

For the marinade, mix all the ingredients together in a shallow dish. Add the beef strips to the marinade and cover. Refrigerate for 1 hour.

For the salad, take a large frying pan (preferably a wok) and heat until very hot. Remove the beef strips from the marinade (reserve the marinade for later). Stir-fry the beef in small batches (a handful at a time) for 2 minutes only. Set aside and keep warm. Add the meat juices from the pan to the marinade. Stir-fry all the vegetables until just soft, then add the meat and marinade and bring to a simmer. Serve on a bed of egg noodles and garnish with parsley.

By Chef Steve – Sanctuary Baines' Camp, Okavango Delta, Botswana

Mediterranean Stuffed Chicken Breast
with a Red Wine Reduction
Serves 4

30 ml sunflower oil
150 g carrots, chopped
100 g green beans, chopped
100 g courgettes (baby marrows), chopped
100 g fresh breadcrumbs
1 egg
pinch each of salt and ground black pepper
1 kg chicken breast fillets
Red Wine Reduction (see page 183) for serving

Heat the oil and fry the carrots, green beans and courgettes until soft. Remove from the pan and place in a mixing bowl. Add the breadcrumbs, egg and seasoning to the vegetable mixture. Flatten out the chicken breast fillets using a meat mallet. Spoon 30 ml of vegetable filling into the centre of each breast fillet and roll up into a sausage shape, sealing the vegetable filling inside. (Secure with toothpicks if necessary to ensure that the filling cannot leak out during cooking.) Wrap each roll of chicken in a piece of foil and twist the ends like a sweet wrapper. Poach the chicken in gently simmering water for 10–12 minutes. Remove the foil carefully and brown the chicken in a nonstick frying pan. Be very gentle as you do not want the chicken to break or split open. Top and tail the chicken sausage and cut into three equal pieces. Serve with your favourite starch and the red wine reduction.

Sanctuary Swala Camp, Tarangire National
Park, Tanzania

Chef Paul's Homemade Chilli Paste

This is an excellent accompaniment to most dishes and should have a regular place at your table. It goes particularly well with crumbed foods, such as prawns, chicken or pork.
Makes 500 g

4 cloves garlic, chopped
3 cm-piece fresh ginger, grated
35 g cumin seeds, toasted
250 g sugar
1 kg red chillies, chopped
750 ml white vinegar

Mix all the ingredients together and bring to a simmer in a saucepan. Simmer for 30 minutes. Pour into a blender and blend until smooth. Return to the heat and reduce until all the liquid has evaporated. Pour into sterilised jars. The chilli paste can be used immediately. Once opened, keep refrigerated and use within one week.

By Chef Paul – Sanctuary Sussi & Chuma, Livingstone, Zambia

Mini Toffee Apples with a Black Cherry Parfait and Homemade Vanilla Ice Cream in Chocolate Baskets

Serves 8

BLACK CHERRY PARFAIT
500 ml fresh cream
35 g icing sugar
30 ml black cherry coulis
   (see page 174)

CHOCOLATE BASKETS
200 g dark chocolate

MINI TOFFEE APPLES
100 g castor sugar
1 Granny Smith apple,
   unpeeled

VANILLA ICE CREAM
500 ml double cream
600 ml full-cream milk
250 g castor sugar
1 vanilla pod, split and scraped
6 egg yolks

For the parfait, pour the cream into a mixing bowl and whisk vigorously while adding the icing sugar until stiff peaks form. Using a spatula, gently fold in the black cherry coulis until combined. Pour into individual serving cups (cappuccino cups work well) and place in the freezer overnight.

For the chocolate baskets, break the chocolate into small pieces and place in a steel mixing bowl suspended over simmering water. Make sure that the bowl does not touch the water. Using a wooden spoon, stir the chocolate continuously until completely melted. Firmly shape a square piece of foil over a mould, making sure there are no gaps in the folds of the foil. Remove the foil and use a teaspoon to line the inside with a layer of melted chocolate. If the chocolate is too runny, allow it to cool slightly until it can form a layer about 3 mm thick. Repeat until you have eight moulds. Place in the fridge to set for 10–20 minutes. Once the chocolate has set you can peel off the foil, leaving you with a chocolate basket. Ensure no pieces of foil are left in the chocolate.

For the mini toffee apples, place the castor sugar in a saucepan and place over medium to low heat. DO NOT STIR. Allow the sugar to melt on its own, giving the saucepan a swirl to move the melted sugar around the bottom of the pan until all the sugar has melted. Reduce to a hard crack stage and remove from the stove. Using a melon baller, scoop eight balls from the apple and place a toothpick firmly in each ball. Allow the sugar to cool slightly then hold the apple by the toothpick and dip it into the caramel. It should come out completely covered. As the caramel hardens, use your fingers (be careful not to burn yourself) to pull the caramel gently from the apple so that it looks like the one in the photograph. This takes some practice, but once you get the hang of it you will end up with a long spear shape.

For the ice cream, place the cream, milk, vanilla seeds, vanilla pod and half the sugar in a heavy-based saucepan over a low heat until the mixture is about to boil. Set aside for 25 minutes. Beat the eggs and the other half of the sugar until pale in colour and ribbon stage is reached. Beat 250 ml of the cream mixture into the egg mixture. Heat up the rest of the cream mixture until just about to boil and then stir in the egg mixture until combined. Return the saucepan to a low heat and stir with a wooden spoon for 10–12 minutes or until the mixture is thick enough to coat the back of a spoon. It is very important that you do not let the mixture boil otherwise you will end up with scrambled eggs. Pour the mixture into a bowl and place inside another bowl of ice water, stirring occasionally until cooled. Discard the vanilla pod and churn the mixture in an ice-cream maker until frozen.

To plate up, fill the chocolate baskets with the vanilla ice cream and serve with the parfait and mini toffee apples.

Rooibos Crème Brûlée

Serves 10

700 ml fresh cream
2 medium or 3 full-flavour tea bags of rooibos tea
zest of 1 orange
8 egg yolks
170 g castor sugar
5 ml vanilla essence

CARAMEL CRUST
50 g castor sugar

Preheat the oven to 170 °C. Place the cream, tea bags and orange zest in a saucepan and heat until just about to boil. Beat the egg yolks with the castor sugar until light and fluffy. Remove the tea bags from the cream mixture and stir the cream into the egg mixture. Add the vanilla essence and pass the mixture through a sieve. Pour the mixture into individual ramekins. Place the ramekins in a roasting pan half-filled with hot water. Bake in the oven for 10 minutes to create a good skin on top. Once cooled, sprinkle the top of the set custard with a thin layer of castor sugar. Using a blowtorch (and being very careful not to burn yourself), melt the sugar until it is golden brown in colour. Refrigerate overnight.

By Chef Gomorena – Sanctuary Stanley's Camp, Okavango Delta, Botswana

Okavango Chocolate Pie

Serves 8

PASTRY
225 g cake flour, plus extra for dusting
30 ml cocoa powder
140 g butter
30 ml castor sugar
15–30 ml cold water

FILLING
175 g butter, at room temperature
350 g brown sugar
4 eggs, lightly beaten
25 g cocoa powder, sifted
150 g plain milk chocolate
300 ml fresh cream

TO DECORATE
425 ml double cream, whipped
chocolate flakes and curls
black cherries and strawberries (optional)

For the pastry, sift the flour and cocoa powder into a mixing bowl. Rub in the butter with your fingertips until the mixture resembles fine breadcrumbs. Stir in the castor sugar and just enough cold water to make a soft dough. Wrap the dough and chill in the fridge for 15 minutes. Preheat the oven to 190 °C. Roll out the pastry on a lightly floured work surface and use it to line a 23 cm loose-based tart pan or ceramic dish. Line with baking paper and fill with baking beans. Bake for 15 minutes. Remove from the oven and take out the beans and baking paper. Bake the pastry case for another 10 minutes. Set aside the pastry case and adjust the oven temperature to 160 °C.

For the filling, beat the butter and brown sugar together in a bowl. Gradually beat in the eggs with the cocoa powder. Melt the chocolate and beat into the mixture along with the single cream. Pour the filling into the pastry case and bake for 45 minutes, or until the filling has set gently. Allow the chocolate pie to cool completely in the pan, then transfer it to a serving plate.

To decorate, cover the pie with the whipped cream and decorate with chocolate flakes and curls. Chill until ready to serve. Decorate with black cherries and strawberries if desired.

Mango and Raspberry Fool
Serves 8

200 g raspberries (fresh or frozen)
170 g castor sugar
250 g mango flesh, diced
500 ml whipped cream, sweetened
fruit of choice and mint for decorating

Toss the raspberries and castor sugar together
in a mixing bowl. Cover and set aside for
45 minutes. Purée the raspberries and mango
in a blender, then pass though a sieve. Pour the
purée into eight dessert glasses, leaving space
for the cream. Top up with the whipped cream
and decorate with fruit and fresh mint.

AFTERNOON TEA

After a longer than planned afternoon snooze it is time for a cup of rooibos tea to awaken those sleepy bones and ready yourself for the afternoon's adventures.

Although afternoon high tea is a very English tradition, it is now also a safari tradition and life just wouldn't be the same without it. Whatever your fancy, whether it be the traditional scone with jam and clotted cream or a more contemporary fruit smoothie, there will definitely be something to your liking.

Dark, Rich Chocolate Cake
Serves 12–15

250 ml water
100 g butter
125 ml sunflower oil
250 g cake flour
25 g cocoa powder
5 ml baking powder
500 g sugar
2 eggs
125 ml milk

TO DECORATE
200 g dark chocolate
100 ml fresh cream

Preheat the oven to 160 °C. Grease a deep baking tray. Pour the water into a small saucepan and bring to a boil. Add the butter and oil to the water and stir until the butter has melted completely. Remove from the heat and set aside to cool. In a separate bowl, sift the flour, cocoa powder, baking powder and sugar together. Add the water mixture to the dry ingredients and mix well. Add the eggs and milk and mix. Pour the cake batter into the prepared baking tray and bake for about 1½ hours, or until a test skewer inserted in the centre comes out clean. Remove from the oven and set aside to cool in the pan.

To decorate, melt the chocolate in a steel bowl suspended over a saucepan of simmering water and then combine with the cream. Pour the chocolate ganache over the cake and smooth out with a spatula. Cut the cake into squares and serve.

Traditional Scones
Makes 12

225 g self-raising flour
pinch of salt
25 g castor sugar
55 g butter, at room temperature
25 ml double cream
1 egg, beaten
100 ml milk

EGG WASH
1 egg, beaten
5 ml water

Preheat the oven to 180 °C. Grease a baking tray. Sift the flour and salt together. Mix in the castor sugar. Mix in the butter until the mixture resembles breadcrumbs. Add the cream, egg and milk. Knead for about 5 minutes or until the dough is smooth. If the dough is too sticky, add a little more flour. Lightly roll out the dough until it is about 2.5 cm thick. Using a ring cutter, cut out rounds and place on the prepared baking tray. Brush the top of the scones with the egg wash. Bake for 15–20 minutes. Serve with jam and whipped cream.

Lemon and Poppy Seed Cake

Serves 8–10

CAKE
60 g poppy seeds
185 ml milk
200 g butter, at room temperature
200 g castor sugar
zest of 1 lemon
3 eggs
400 g self-raising flour
250 ml freshly squeezed lemon juice

LEMON SYRUP
250 g sugar
250 ml freshly squeezed lemon juice
zest of 2 medium lemons

For the cake, preheat the oven to 180 °C. Line the base and sides of a 20 cm cake tin with baking paper. Mix the poppy seeds and milk in a mixing bowl. In a separate mixing bowl, beat the butter, castor sugar and lemon zest until creamy. Add the eggs, one at a time, beating well after each addition. Sift the flour into the egg mixture while beating. Add the lemon juice and the milk mixture. When everything is well mixed, spoon the batter into the prepared cake tin. Bake for 45 minutes, or until a test skewer inserted into the centre comes out clean.

For the syrup, place the sugar, lemon juice and zest in a saucepan over a low heat until the sugar has dissolved. Reduce until the liquid forms a syrup. Pour half of the hot syrup over the cake as soon as it comes out the oven. Allow the cake to cool, then pour the rest of the syrup over the cake until just covered. Slice and serve.

Smoked Salmon and Cream Cheese on Cucumber Rounds

Makes 12 portions

80 g sour cream
80 g cream cheese
salt and ground black pepper
1 cucumber, sliced into 12 rounds about 5 mm thick
125 g sliced smoked salmon, cut into 12 strips about 1 cm wide
sprigs fresh dill for garnishing

Combine the sour cream and cream cheese in a bowl and stir well. Season to taste with salt and pepper. Place the cucumber rounds neatly on a platter. Roll up the salmon strips and place them on the cucumber, slightly to one side. Using two teaspoons, shape quenelles with the cream cheese mixture. Place a quenelle next to the smoked salmon. Refrigerate until ready to serve. Garnish each cucumber round with a sprig of dill.

Rooibos Iced Tea
Serves 6

5 rooibos tea bags
1 lemon, sliced
15–20 mint leaves
1.5 litres boiling water
castor sugar to taste (optional)

Place the tea bags, lemon slices and mint leaves in a large teapot. Pour in the boiling water and allow the mixture to brew. When the tea is as strong as you like it, remove the tea bags and strain the tea. Add castor sugar to taste. Allow to cool, then refrigerate. Serve with plenty of ice.

Homemade Lemonade
Serves 6

300 ml water
250 g sugar
250 ml freshly squeezed lemon juice
additional 700 ml water to dilute

Bring the 300 ml water to a boil in a small saucepan and add the sugar. Stir until the sugar has dissolved completely. Remove from the heat and add the lemon juice. Add enough cold water to dilute it according to your taste. Allow to cool completely, then refrigerate. Serve with plenty of ice and a slice of lemon.

Sanctuary Olonana Safari Camp, Masai Mara National Park, Kenya

AFTERNOON DRIVE AND SUNDOWNERS

Sanctuary Chobe Chilwero, Chobe River,
Chobe National Park, Botswana

The guide rounds up everyone and ushers you onto the game drive or sunset cruiser. There are spectacular beauties waiting and time is precious.

I am not sure where or when it started, but we have a safari tradition that is practised religiously. It involves a salute to the setting sun and a celebration of another glorious day in Africa coming to an end. The fondly known 'sundowner' usually involves a glass of your favourite tipple and a handful of moreish snacks that you somehow seem to find space for. One thing is for sure though, it needs no arm-twisting to ensure a healthy attendance to this timeless gathering.

Once the sun has set and the darkness begins to creep in, it is time for another adventure. This time, a hunt for the creatures of the night. And if you are lucky, which you usually are, a hunting predator will cross your path before your search is over.

Malawi Shandy Summer Cooler
Makes 1

1 tot passion fruit (granadilla) cordial
dash of bitters
200 ml lemonade
200 ml ginger ale
½ tot grenadine
1 slice orange for garnishing

Pour the passion fruit cordial into a tall glass. Add the bitters. Fill the glass
with ice. Pour in the lemonade and ginger ale. Carefully pour in the grenadine —
it will sink to the bottom of the glass and give great presentation.
Garnish with the orange slice.

Caramelised Groundnuts
Makes about 375 g

120 ml water
375 g sugar
375 g groundnuts (or raw unsalted peanuts)

Prepare a baking tray lined with foil. Place the water and sugar in a saucepan and bring to a
simmer over medium heat. Keep stirring and reduce until the mixture reaches syrup stage.
Add the groundnuts and keep stirring until the mixture crystallises and the nuts are completely
coated. Reduce the heat and keep stirring. The sugar will melt and caramelise. Keep stirring until
the caramel darkens. Do not let the sugar darken too much or it will taste bitter. Pour out onto
the baking tray and spread out in an even layer. Allow to cool completely. Break the nuts apart
and store in an airtight container until needed.

Chillied Groundnuts

Makes about 250 g

- 250 g groundnuts (or raw unsalted peanuts)
- 30 ml lemon juice
- 30 ml chilli powder
- 5 ml salt
- 1 ml cayenne pepper

Preheat the oven to 120 °C. Mix all the ingredients together in a bowl. Spread the mixture in an even layer on a baking tray and bake for about 1 hour, or until dried. Stir every 10–15 minutes. Allow to cool before storing in an airtight container.

Red Mamba Cocktail

Makes 1

1½ tots vodka
1 tot Campari
½ tot Simple Syrup (see below)
1 tot red cranberry juice
5 ice cubes

Place all the ingredients in a cocktail shaker and shake well for about 10 seconds. Pour into a chilled martini glass with a slice of orange as a garnish.

Simple Syrup

Makes about 250 ml

250 ml water
250 ml sugar

Bring the water to a boil and then take off the heat. Add the sugar and stir until it has dissolved. Pour into a clean container and refrigerate until well chilled. The syrup can be stored for up to two weeks in the fridge.

CANAPÉS

Santuary Puku Ridge Camp, South Luangwa National Park, Zambia

All too soon you are back at camp. After a quick shower under the stars there is time to squeeze in a pre-dinner drink and a few more delectable tidbits. Again, no arm-twisting required. There seems to be delicious food around every corner, but no one is complaining.

There is nothing better than that moment when you're sitting around the fire and sharing the experiences of the day: how close you got to that lion and who was lucky enough to see that pack of wilds dogs on the hunt. It is truly remarkable when you realise how much you have seen in one day. As you sit and contemplate and slowly take it all in, you are mesmerised by the dancing flames, and for a moment you are nowhere and everywhere all at the same time.

Beetroot and Soft Cheese Samoosas
Makes 10–12

40 ml sunflower oil
½ onion, finely chopped
2 cloves garlic, crushed and chopped
8 beetroot, cooked and chopped
1 chilli, finely chopped
30 ml lemon juice
pinch of salt
125 g Camembert cheese, cut into small pieces
1 roll ready-made samoosa pastry
cooking oil for deep-frying

Heat the sunflower oil in a frying pan and sauté the onion and garlic until the garlic begins to brown. Add the beetroot, chilli and lemon juice to the pan and season with salt. Cook the mixture over a low heat until soft. Place a teaspoonful of the beetroot mixture and a few pieces of the Camembert in the centre of a strip of the pastry and fold into a triangle. Repeat until all the filling is used up. Deep-fry the samoosas until the pastry is golden brown. Remove with a slotted spoon and place on paper towels to absorb excess oil. Serve hot.

Lemon and Chilli Olives

Serves 4–6

10 ml vegetable oil
1 x 350 g tin pitted black or green olives
10 ml chopped fresh rosemary
1 clove garlic, finely chopped
1 chilli, chopped
juice of 1 lemon
chopped fresh parsley for serving (optional)

Heat the oil in a frying pan over medium heat. Mix the olives, rosemary, garlic, chilli and lemon juice together and pan-fry for 10–15 minutes. Place in small serving bowls or skewer each olive on the end of a toothpick and serve sprinkled with chopped fresh parsley if desired.

Sun-dried Tomato Pinwheels
Serves 8

1 x 400 g roll ready-made puff pastry
80 g sun-dried tomatoes, chopped
50 g Cheddar cheese, grated

Preheat the oven to 200 °C. Line a baking tray with baking paper. Roll out the pastry to a thickness of 3–4 mm. Spread the sun-dried tomatoes over the pastry in an even layer. Sprinkle with Cheddar cheese. Roll each end of the puff pastry towards the centre until both rolled ends meet in the middle. Slightly pinch the rolled ends together so that they won't unravel while baking. Using a sharp knife, slice the roll into roughly 1-cm-thick slices. Place the slices on the prepared baking tray and bake in the oven for 20 minutes, or until golden and crisp. Serve immediately.

Sanctuary Puku Ridge Camp, South Luangwa National Park, Zambia

DINNER

Sanctuary Chief's Camp, Okavango Delta, Botswana

While you are all enjoying yourselves just a little too much around the fireplace, your waiter appears with a twinkle in his eye and a wry smile. You know what this means; like the slow-moving wildebeest of the Serengeti, everyone migrates to the dinner table.

More often than not, a safari dinner is a communal affair because everyone enjoys sharing their stories around the dinner table. You are also graciously hosted by your guide, who always has some interesting 'bush tales' to share.

With service comparable to any five-star experience, your wine glass stays full and your three-course meal is beautifully presented.

Crumbed Camembert on Beetroot Carpaccio with a Beetroot Coulis

Serves 6

BEETROOT COULIS
2 cloves garlic
3 medium beetroot, cooked, peeled and chopped
45 ml olive oil

CRUMBED CAMEMBERT
125 g Camembert cheese
70 g flour
1 egg, beaten
120 g dried breadcrumbs
cooking oil for deep-frying

TO PLATE UP
4 medium beetroot, cooked, peeled and sliced 2 mm thick
6 rocket leaves
deep-fried rice noodles for garnishing
45 ml Sweet Chilli Sauce (see page 182)

For the beetroot coulis, purée the garlic, beetroot and olive oil in a food processor until smooth. Set aside.

For the crumbed Camembert, cut the cheese into six equal wedges. Place the flour, egg and breadcrumbs into three separate small bowls. Using one wedge at a time, coat the Camembert in flour, then dip into the egg and finally roll in the breadcrumbs. The cheese should be completely coated in breadcrumbs. Set aside for 15 minutes to set. Heat the oil in a deep saucepan and deep-fry the Camembert, three pieces at a time. Do not cook for too long or the crumb coating will break and the Camembert will leak out. Lift the Camembert out of the oil with a slotted spoon and place on paper towels to absorb the excess oil. Serve immediately while the Camembert is still piping hot.

To plate up, layer five slices of beetroot neatly in the centre of each plate. Place a rocket leaf on top of the beetroot, but do not cover it completely. Place a Camembert wedge on the rocket. Garnish with a few deep-fried noodles. Drizzle the beetroot coulis and sweet chilli sauce around the plate.

Celery and Onion Soup
Serves 4

10 ml butter
400 g celery, chopped
700 g onions, chopped
700 ml vegetable stock
350 ml water
pinch each of salt and ground black pepper

Melt the butter in a deep saucepan and sauté the celery and onions until just soft. Add the stock and water and bring to a simmer for 15 minutes. Season to taste and set aside to cool. Once cooled, blend until smooth and pass through a sieve. Return to the saucepan and bring back to a simmer. Season again and serve.

Couscous-crusted Prawns with a Sweet Chilli Sauce

Serves 4

COUSCOUS-CRUSTED PRAWNS

50 g cake flour
pinch of ground black pepper
12 prawns, peeled and deveined (leave tails intact)
2 eggs, beaten
100 g couscous, cooked
150 ml cooking oil for deep-frying
salad leaves for serving

SWEET CHILLI SAUCE

(see page 182)

For the couscous-crusted prawns, season the flour with black pepper. Dust each prawn in the seasoned flour, then dip into the beaten eggs and finally roll in the cooked couscous. Coat well to ensure there are no gaps. Set aside for about 15 minutes to allow the coating to set. Deep-fry the prawns in hot oil for about 2 minutes per side.

To plate up, place a few salad leaves in the centre of each plate and top with three prawns. Drizzle with the sweet chilli sauce.

Crumbed Aubergine with Mozzarella, Kiwi Pesto and Caper Sauce

Serves 8

pinch each of salt and ground black pepper
200 g cake flour
8 round aubergine (brinjal) slices, 5 mm thick
3 eggs, beaten
200 g dried breadcrumbs
100 ml vegetable oil
8 round mozzarella slices, 6 cm in diameter
8 sprigs fresh rosemary
8 slices tomato
8 large sweet basil leaves or sprigs

CAPER SAUCE
see page 182

KIWI PESTO
see page 182

Add the seasoning to the flour. One by one, coat the aubergine slices in the flour, then dip into the beaten eggs and finally coat in the breadcrumbs. Set aside for about 15 minutes to allow the coating to set. Heat the oil in a saucepan; the oil should be at least 2 cm deep. Deep-fry the crumbed aubergine slices, two at a time, until golden brown. If you add too many at once the oil will cool down and the aubergine will absorb too much oil. Remove the aubergine slices with a slotted spoon and place on some paper towels to absorb the excess oil.

To plate up, create a stack of mozzarella, aubergine, rosemary, tomato and basil on each plate. Spoon over some caper sauce and drizzle the pesto on the plate.

Smoked Salmon Salad with a Lemon Dressing

Serves 4

150 g smoked salmon (the best quality you can afford)
30 ml Lemon Dressing (see page 180)

POTATO SALAD
½ red pepper
½ yellow pepper
45 ml mayonnaise
3 medium potatoes
pinch each of salt and ground black pepper
4 sprigs fresh flat-leaf parsley for garnishing

For the potato salad, preheat the oven to 120 °C. Place the red and yellow peppers on a well-oiled baking tray and roast for 20 minutes until soft. Place in a plastic bag and leave to sweat for 10 minutes (this will make it much easier to peel the peppers). Peel, dice and combine the peppers with the mayonnaise. Boil the potatoes in salted water for about 30 minutes, or until tender. Set aside to cool. Once cooled, peel and dice the potatoes and combine with the mayonnaise and peppers. Season to taste.

To plate up, use a ring cutter of about 5 cm in diameter, and portion out the smoked salmon on a cutting board before transferring to each plate. Using a smaller ring cutter of about 2 cm in diameter, neatly mould the potato salad on top (and in the centre) of the smoked salmon. Garnish the potato salad with the fresh parsley and drizzle the lemon dressing around the salmon. Serve immediately.

Red Wine-braised Lamb Shank
with Oven-roasted Root Vegetables
Serves 4

LAMB SHANKS
4 lamb shanks
10 ml olive oil
20 ml balsamic vinegar
125 ml good red wine
4 sprigs fresh rosemary
10 cloves garlic, unpeeled
cooking oil for frying
4 small onions, chopped
3 tomatoes, grated
1 x 400 g tin whole peeled tomatoes
pinch each of salt and ground black pepper

VEGETABLES
2 large carrots
2 large parsnips
2 medium red onions
½ butternut
15 ml olive oil
7.5 ml chopped fresh mixed herbs

For the lamb shanks, marinate them overnight in the olive oil, vinegar, red wine, rosemary and garlic. Remove the lamb shanks from the marinade (reserve the marinade for later). Heat some cooking oil in a large saucepan and brown the lamb shanks. Add the onions and fry until soft. Add the marinade and deglaze the saucepan. Add the grated and tinned tomatoes and simmer for about 2 hours, or until the lamb is tender and barely attached to the bone. Season to taste.

For the vegetables, preheat the oven to 180 °C. Peel and cut all the vegetables into bite-sized pieces. Toss the vegetables with the olive oil and herbs. Spread the vegetables in an even layer on a baking tray. Roast in the oven until fork-tender. Give the vegetables a good toss every 5 minutes or so.

Serve the shanks and vegetables on a bed of couscous to soak up the sauce.

Grilled Eland Steak with a Port and Chocolate Sauce served with Polenta Cakes and Oven-roasted Vegetables

Serves 2

ELAND STEAK

400 g eland fillet (or beef fillet)

100 ml olive oil

2.5 ml ground cloves

2.5 ml paprika

2.5 ml ground coriander

pinch each of salt and ground black pepper

15 ml cooking oil

POLENTA CAKES

260 g instant polenta (cornmeal)

1.5 litres vegetable stock

salt and ground black pepper

40 g butter

70 g finely grated Parmesan cheese

40 g cake flour

60 ml olive oil

OVEN-ROASTED VEGETABLES

30 ml chopped fresh thyme

30 ml chopped fresh rosemary

60 ml olive oil

salt and ground black pepper

1 red pepper, cut into strips

1 green pepper, cut into strips

1 red onion, sliced

1 large carrot, peeled and cut into strips

3 courgettes, cut into strips

PORT AND CHOCOLATE SAUCE

25 g butter

15 ml chopped onion

180 ml beef stock

120 ml Port

5 ml chopped fresh mixed herbs

50 g dark chocolate, grated

For the eland steak, marinate the meat in the oil, cloves, paprika, coriander, salt and pepper for at least 1 hour. (While the meat is marinating, roast the sweet potato.) To cook the steak, heat the oil in a frying pan until the pan starts smoking. Remove the eland fillet from the marinade and cut into 200 g steaks. Seal the steak on all sides and cook to your liking.

For the polenta cakes, grease a baking tray with olive oil. Mix the polenta with the stock in a saucepan until well combined. Place over a medium heat and bring almost to a boil. Reduce the heat and simmer gently until thick. If the mixture becomes too thick, add water. Season to taste. While the mixture is still hot, pour it into the prepared tray. Spread out to an even 1cm thick layer. Cover with plastic wrap and place in the fridge for about 2 hours. Preheat the oven to 190 °C. Cut the polenta into 12 squares and bake until the outer edges begin to brown..

For the vegetables, preheat the oven to 240 °C. In a bowl, stir the thyme, rosemary, olive oil, salt, and pepper together. Mix well with the vegetables and spread out in a large roasting pan. Roast for 15–20 minutes, tossing every 5 minutes, or until vegetables are cooked.

For the sauce, melt the butter in a saucepan and sauté the onion for 3 minutes. Add the stock, Port and herbs and reduce for 3 minutes. Remove from the heat and whisk in the chocolate until it melts and thickens the sauce.

To plate up, place the sauce in a small piping bag and 'draw' the sauce onto the plate using a zigzag pattern. Place a polenta cake in the centre of the plate and top with the vegetables and steak.

By Chef Phinias – Sanctuary Chobe Chilwero, Chobe National Park, Botswana

Kudu Kebabs with Red Wine Cranberry Sauce

Serves 8

KEBABS

800 g kudu fillet, cubed (or beef fillet)
4 bay leaves
4 basil leaves, chopped
120 ml vegetable oil
30 ml coarse salt
45 ml ready-made cranberry sauce
8 bamboo skewers
sprigs of parsley for garnishing

RED WINE CRANBERRY SAUCE

300 ml good red wine
300 ml water
150 g butter, diced
150 g ready-made cranberry sauce
15 ml brown sugar
salt and ground black pepper

For the kebabs, place the cubes of kudu in a large mixing bowl and add the bay leaves, basil, oil, salt and cranberry sauce. Stir well until combined. Marinate overnight. (Soak the skewers in water before adding the meat and grilling as this will stop the kebabs from burning.) Skewer three cubes of meat onto each skewer. Grill the skewers on a high heat for 8–10 minutes, turning occasionally. Allow to rest for a few minutes before serving.

For the sauce, simmer the wine and water in a saucepan until reduced by half. Whisk in the diced butter one cube at a time until the sauce becomes glossy. Stir in the cranberry sauce. Add the brown sugar and salt and pepper to taste.

Serve the kebabs with the sauce spooned over, and a starch and vegetables of your choice.

By Chef Harry – Sanctuary Chief's Camp, Okavango Delta, Botswana

Pan-seared Duck Breast with a Mushroom and Red Wine Sauce and Creamy Mashed Potatoes

Serves 4

DUCK
4 duck breasts
10 ml cooking oil

MUSHROOM AND RED WINE SAUCE
40 g butter
1 onion, chopped
85 g button mushrooms, sliced
125 ml good red wine
500 ml beef stock
pinch each of salt and ground black pepper

CREAMY MASHED POTATOES
1.6 kg potatoes, washed, peeled and chopped
40 g butter
5 ml Dijon mustard
125 ml thickened cream
125 ml milk
salt and ground black pepper

For the duck, score the skin of the breasts. (This is to stop the breasts from curling during the cooking process.) Heat the oil in a pan until sizzling hot. Place the duck breasts in the pan, skin side down, and fry until the skin is crispy. This will take about 4 minutes. Turn the duck breasts over and cook to your liking. Set aside to rest for 10 minutes.

For the sauce, use the same pan in which you cooked the duck. Add the butter, onion and mushrooms and sauté until the onion is soft. Deglaze the pan with the red wine. Add the stock and bring to a simmer. Reduce until thick enough to coat the back of a spoon. Strain the sauce and season to taste.

For the mash, place the potatoes in cold water and bring to a boil over a high heat. Boil until tender and then drain the potatoes. Return the potatoes to the saucepan and cook out some of the moisture. Take off the heat and mash the potatoes until smooth. Add the butter, mustard, cream and milk and use a wooden spoon to combine. Press the mash through a sieve. Season to taste.

To plate up, carve the duck breast into even slices of about 1 cm thick. Place a dollop of mashed potato in the centre of the plate and neatly arrange the duck slices around the mash. Drizzle the sauce around the outer edge of the duck breast and serve immediately.

Crocodile Curry

Serves 6

60 ml olive oil
1 kg crocodile tail, cubed
1 onion, chopped
3 large cloves garlic, crushed
3 cm-piece fresh ginger, grated
5 ml cumin seeds
5 ml turmeric
500 ml chicken stock
15 ml tomato paste
15 ml red curry paste
125 ml coconut milk
30 ml chopped fresh coriander
pinch each of salt and ground black pepper
200 g basmati rice, cooked, and poppadom baskets for serving

Heat half of the olive oil in a frying pan. Fry the crocodile cubes for 2 minutes and then set aside. Heat the rest of the olive oil in a saucepan and sauté the onion, garlic, ginger, cumin seeds and turmeric for 2 minutes. Add the chicken stock and bring to a boil for 5–10 minutes. Add the crocodile cubes, tomato paste and red curry paste and cook for 10 minutes. Add the coconut milk and fresh coriander. Season to taste and serve in a poppadom basket on a mound of basmati rice. Serve with a sambal of your choice.

By Chef Paul – Sanctuary Sussi & Chuma, Livingstone, Zambia

No-bake Cheesecake with Cherry Compote

Serves 10

CRUST
150 g Tennis® biscuits
85 g butter

FILLING
500 g cream cheese
500 ml fresh cream
2 x 400 g tins condensed milk
120 ml lemon juice
zest of 1 lemon
2.5 ml vanilla essence

CHERRY COMPOTE
200 g fresh cherries (or tinned if you cannot find fresh)
80 g castor sugar
250 ml water (or the juice from the tin if using tinned cherries)
60 ml Port

For the crust, prepare 10 individual ramekins by lining them with foil. This will make the desserts very easy to unmould before serving. Crush the biscuits in a food processor until a fine crumb consistency. If you don't have a processor, an easy way to crush the biscuits is with a rolling pin while still in the packet (be careful not to break the packet in the process). Melt the butter and combine with the biscuit crumbs. Line each ramekin with a thin layer (about 2 mm thick) of biscuit crumbs, using a dessert spoon to compress the crust and obtain a smooth finish. Place in the fridge to set.

For the filling, combine the cream cheese, cream and condensed milk in an electric mixer and mix until smooth. Add the lemon juice, lemon zest and vanilla essence. Pour the cheesecake filling into the prepared crusts and place in the fridge to set for about 1 hour. Remove the cheesecakes from the ramekins and carefully peel off the foil.

For the cherry compote, place all the ingredients in a saucepan and reduce until thick enough to coat the back of a spoon.

To plate up, place the cheesecake in the centre of the plate and spoon the cherry compote over the top and in a drizzle around the cheesecake.

Forest Berry Roll

Serves 12

SPONGE BASE

6 eggs, separated
220 g castor sugar
55 ml water
15 ml freshly squeezed lemon juice
15 ml lemon zest
220 g cake flour
2.5 ml cream of tartar
1 ml salt
100 g icing sugar for dusting

FILLING

200 ml double cream
100 g icing sugar
zest of 1 lemon
700 g frozen berries

For the sponge base, preheat the oven to 160 °C. Line a baking tray with greaseproof paper. Beat the egg yolks in a heatproof bowl suspended over a saucepan of simmering water until very thick and creamy in colour. Beat the castor sugar into the egg yolks, one teaspoon at a time. (This is called a *sabayon*.) Add the water, lemon juice and lemon zest. Beat in the flour. In a separate mixing bowl, beat the egg whites until light and frothy. Add the cream of tartar and salt. Beat the mixture until the egg whites reach stiff peak stage, but aren't dry. Fold the egg white mixture into the egg yolk mixture. Pour the batter into the prepared baking tray and bake for 1 hour. Remove the baking tray from the oven and turn upside down onto a clean, dry dishcloth that has been dusted with icing sugar to stop the base from sticking to the cloth. Roll up the sponge base in the dishcloth and set aside to cool.

For the filling, pour the cream into a large mixing bowl and beat until stiff. Whisk in the icing sugar and the lemon zest. Add the berries and fold in. Unroll the sponge base, peel off the greaseproof paper and spread the filling evenly over the sponge. With the long side of the sponge rectangle facing you, and using the dishcloth, carefully roll up the cake again.

Chocolate Truffle Tart with a Cherry Coulis

Serves 8

TART
350 g Tennis® biscuits
70 g butter
400 g dark chocolate (70% cocoa)
400 ml fresh cream
sprigs fresh mint for garnishing

CHERRY COULIS
2 x 400 g tins pitted cherries
250 ml berry juice
60 ml sugar

For the tart, set aside eight ring moulds about 8 cm high and with a 5 cm diameter. Cut eight pieces of foil into strips measuring 4 cm x 20 cm and use to line the inside of the moulds. Crush the biscuits in a food processor or blender until fine. Melt the butter and combine with the biscuit crumbs. Spoon one heaped tablespoon of biscuit crumbs into the bottom of each mould and press flat to form a biscuit base. Melt the chocolate in a heatproof bowl suspended over a saucepan of simmering water, being careful not to overheat the chocolate. Mix the melted chocolate with the cream and pour the chocolate mixture into the moulds. Place the moulds in the fridge for 1 hour to set. Carefully push the chocolate tarts out of the moulds, pushing from the bottom up. Remove the foil carefully, making sure no pieces are left in the chocolate.

For the coulis, drain the cherries from the tin and reserve about a quarter of the juice. Place the cherries and juice in a blender and blend until smooth. Press though a fine sieve and place in a saucepan. Bring to a simmer and add the berry juice and sugar. Simmer until thick enough to coat the back of a spoon.

To plate up, place the coulis in a small piping bag and 'draw' the coulis onto the plate using a zigzag pattern. Place the chocolate tart in the centre of the plate and garnish with fresh mint.

An aerial view of Sanctuary Baines Camp

OTHER RECIPES

A relaxing afternoon spent in the Okavango Delta on a traditional Makoro

Over the next few pages you will find some basic recipes for various accompaniments that can be served with a variety of dishes, to add an extra dimension and balance of flavour.

Onion Marmalade
Makes about 1.5 litres (3 x 500 ml jars)

    75 ml olive oil
    2 kg onions, sliced lengthways
    225 g white sugar
    125 g dark brown sugar
    500 ml red wine
    250 ml balsamic vinegar
    10 ml salt

Heat the olive oil in a large saucepan. Add the onions and cook over a low heat for 25 minutes, or until the onions turn golden brown. Add the sugars, red wine, balsamic vinegar and salt. Reduce until the liquid has completely evaporated. To test, drag a wooden spoon though the mixture and it should leave a deep channel. Remove from the heat and allow to cool. Pour into sterilised jars, seal and refrigerate. Once opened, the marmalade will keep for about one week.

Lemon Dressing
Makes about 375 ml

    250 ml freshly squeezed lemon juice
    5 ml salt
    2.5 ml ground black pepper
    125 ml extra virgin olive oil

Place the lemon juice, salt and pepper in a blender. Blend on a slow speed while adding the olive oil, drop by drop, until emulsified. This dressing will keep in the fridge for 4–5 days.

Preserved Oranges
Makes 1 large jar

    2 medium oranges, washed and dried
    100 g salt
    125 ml freshly squeezed lemon juice
    125 ml freshly squeezed orange juice

For the preserved oranges, slice the oranges crossways, each slice about 3 mm thick . Place the orange slices in a plastic bag and freeze overnight. Remove the orange slices from the plastic bag and refrigerate for about 4 hours to thaw slightly. Place orange slices in a bowl and add salt. Stir until orange slices are coated in salt. Place the orange slices and salt from bowl into a sterilised jar., and add the lemon and orange juice. Seal the jar and shake. Store in a cool, dark place for one month.

Cucumber Raita
Makes about 250 ml

5 ml cumin seeds
½ cucumber, grated or finely chopped
250 ml plain yoghurt
30 mint leaves, chopped
pinch of salt

Lightly toast the cumin seeds in a dry cast-iron frying pan or heavy-bottomed saucepan. Squeeze out all the excess juice from the cucumber. Mix all the ingredients together well. Chill before serving.

Homemade Chutney
Makes about 1 litre (2 x 500 ml jars)

320 g green apples, peeled, cored and grated
160 g onions, grated
1 kg underripe tomatoes, chopped
180 g sultanas
20 g garlic, chopped
180 g sugar
pinch of salt
350 ml cider vinegar
2.5 ml cayenne pepper
5 ml mustard powder

Place all the ingredients in a large saucepan and bring to a simmer. Reduce the mixture to a thick consistency. Test by drawing a wooden spoon through the mixture. If it does not fill immediately with liquid then the chutney is ready. Pour into sterilised jars. Once opened, the chutney will keep in the fridge for 1–2 weeks.

Balsamic Reduction
Makes 125 ml

270 ml good quality balsamic vinegar
80 ml honey

Place the vinegar and honey in a saucepan and reduce over medium heat until thick and sticky.

Kiwi Pesto
Makes 150 ml

30 g pine kernels
16 sweet basil leaves
2 kiwi fruits, peeled and chopped
50 ml white balsamic vinegar
50 ml olive oil
10 ml soy sauce
dollop of honey
salt and ground black pepper to taste

Roast the pine kernels in a dry frying pan. Take care that they don't burn. Place the pine kernels and remaining ingredients in a blender or food processor and blend until smooth. Check seasoning and blend for another 10 seconds. Use immediately.

Caper Sauce
Makes 250 ml

150 g capers in vinegar
3 eggs, hard-boiled and chopped
8 gherkins, chopped
60 ml mayonnaise
30 ml sour cream

Place all the ingredients in a small bowl and stir to combine. Cover the bowl and marinate in the fridge for 3 hours. Serve immediately. Do not keep for more than 24 hours.

Sweet Chilli Sauce
Makes 1 litre (2 x 500 ml jars)

500 ml white vinegar
400 g white sugar
150 ml fish sauce
120 ml sherry
30 ml chopped red chillies
6 cloves garlic, chopped

Place all the ingredients in a saucepan and bring to a simmer. Allow to reduce by one-third until thick. Set aside to cool and then pour into a sterilised jar. Once opened, this sauce will keep in the fridge for up to one week.

Red Wine Reduction
Makes 350 ml

750 ml good red wine
125 g sugar
2 bay leaves
½ carrot
½ onion

Place all the ingredients in a saucepan and bring to a simmer. Reduce until the liquid reaches a syrup stage. Watch it very closely as it can easily burn if it reduces too much. Strain through a sieve and use immediately or store in the fridge for 3–4 days. Reheat before serving.

Basic Danish Pastry
Makes about 1 kg

460 g butter, at room temperature
650 g cake flour
30 ml instant yeast
425 ml milk
100 g sugar
2 large eggs
15 ml lemon zest
15 ml almond essence

Cream the butter and 90 g of the flour together. Divide into six balls of equal size. Wrap each ball in greaseproof paper and refrigerate. In a large mixing bowl, mix the yeast and 500 g sifted flour together. In a large saucepan, heat the milk and sugar until lukewarm. Whisk the warm milk mixture into the yeast mixture and stir in the eggs, lemon zest and almond essence. Mix for 5 minutes. Transfer the mixture to a work surface and knead in the remaining 60 g flour until the dough is firm. Set aside in a warm place until the dough has doubled in size. Cut the dough in half and roll each half into a square. Remove three of the cold butterballs from the fridge and discard the greaseproof paper. Thinly slice the butterballs. Lay the cold butterball slices on top of the squares of dough and fold the dough over the butter as if you are closing a book. Press the edges together with your fingers to seal. Roll out each piece into a rectangle and then fold into thirds. Wrap in plastic wrap and refrigerate for 30 minutes. Roll out the dough into a rectangle again and fold into thirds.

Repeat this process with the remaining three butterballs. Once all the butter has been incorporated, the dough is ready to use. Ensure that the pastry remains cold while you work with it.

IN CLOSING

With a final nightcap back at the fireplace and the warmth of the fire being enjoyed by the last few stragglers, you wonder, what tomorrow will bring?

I guess this is what makes a safari so special. Every day is a new adventure and you're already planning your next trip before you come to the end of this one. Perhaps Uganda to come face-to-face with a silverback gorilla? Or maybe Botswana, where you will drift silently though the magical Okavango Delta? One thing is for sure though, safari gets into your bones and once you've been smitten it will turn into a lifelong love affair.

THE CAMPS

Zambia

Sanctuary Zebra Plains Camp
This is one of our wildest camps and it is run entirely on solar energy. There isn't a single road in the area, except for the one that takes you to camp. Zebra Plains is a dedicated walking camp that is an exhilarating way to experience the wild animals of Africa.

When it comes to the Zebra Plains kitchen, Moffat is the man in charge. He is an expert with a wood stove and a 'ground oven', and it is truly incredible what he can pull out of his chef's hat with the most basic kitchen at his disposal.

Sanctuary Puku Ridge Camp
Sanctuary Puku Ridge Camp is nestled in a remote game-rich area of South Luangwa National Park. This traditional tented camp has a very intimate atmosphere, and combines an authentic safari experience under canvas, with panoramic views over the abundant flood plain below. Each of the seven oversized tents has picture-windows and a private, decked balcony.

Sanctuary Chichele Presidential Lodge
This historic property, once the personal retreat of former Zambian President, Kenneth Kaunda, has a magnificent hilltop location in Zambia's South Luangwa National Park. Carefully restored to preserve its turn-of-the-century elegance, Sanctuary Chichele Presidential Lodge is approached through a majestic arched entrance leading to a huge colonial-style lounge. The lodge is accessible year-round and is an ideal base for exploring the prolific wildlife in the area.

Sanctuary Sussi & Chuma
Sanctuary Sussi & Chuma is named after Victorian explorer Dr David Livingstone's two faithful companions. Comprising two private Chuma houses and a stunning luxury lodge, Sanctuary Sussi & Chuma is situated along one of the most beautiful stretches of the Zambezi on a lush, fast-flowing bend in the river. The main lodge consists of a unique two-storey lounge and dining area. The second floor bar has an elegant shaded deck, with incredible bird's-eye views across the Zambezi.

Botswana

Sanctuary Baines' Camp

Located on the Boro River, this camp is set amongst the shady trees and water of the Okavango Delta, in a private concession bordering the Moremi Game Reserve. The camp, named after the famous nineteenth-century explorer, Thomas Baines, features five luxurious suites set on elevated platforms in the tree line, with wooden decks that offer expansive views over the permanent water of the river and a lagoon teeming with life.

Sanctuary Stanley's Camp

Sanctuary Stanley's Camp sits amidst 260 000 acres of untamed African bush in a private concession. Bordering the southern section of the famous Moremi Game Reserve, Stanley's is a small luxury camp consisting of eight classic-styled safari tents. Each tent features en-suite facilities and a private balcony, while the main building offers expansive views over the surrounding flood plains.

Sanctuary Chief's Camp

Sanctuary Chief's Camp is a luxury camp on Chief's Island in the exclusive Mombo Concession of the Moremi Game Reserve. This area is considered to have the finest game viewing in southern Africa, including the Big Five. Guest accommodation comprises 12 secluded, permanent luxury bush pavilions. The main deck area is split-level and offers expansive views over the flood plain, while the lower level of the deck houses an exquisite swimming pool.

Sanctuary Chobe Chilwero

Sanctuary Chobe Chilwero borders Chobe National Park. It is set on a hill above the Chobe River and offers unparalleled panoramic views across the islands and flood plains, as far as neighbouring Namibia. Accommodation is in 15 air-conditioned cottages and the main public area includes a lounge and dining room, which are linked to outdoor viewing patios. Sanctuary Chobe Chilwero also boasts a full spa.

Tanzania

Sanctuary Kusini

Perfectly sited in a cluster of rocky outcrops, Sanctuary Kusini's 12 spacious tents blend seamlessly into the predator-rich plains of the Serengeti. Part of Sanctuary Kusini's charm is its remote and private location within the park, offering exceptional and essentially private game viewing. The Serengeti is home to the great wildebeest migration and the short-grass plains provide the perfect setting for the wildebeest as they mass around the area in the early months of each year.

Sanctuary Swala Camp

This camp is located in an exceptionally private section of the Tarangire National Park, and offers visitors a luxurious and exclusive safari experience. Elephant, in particular, love to come to the camp to drink at the water hole; and the big cats are often seen amongst the massive baobab trees.

Sanctuary Saadani River Lodge

Sanctuary Saadani River Lodge is our newest river retreat, with 17 stilted suites hidden within the trees bordering the Wami River. The views from the lodge allow guests to watch the local wildlife while enjoying breakfast, lunch and dinner.

Sanctuary Saadani Safari Lodge

Sanctuary Saadani Safari Lodge is set on the coast of Tanzania, where you can experience untamed, untouched East Africa combined with the beauty of the Indian Ocean. The lodge has six eco-friendly suites, each with ocean views opening onto the white sand beaches, and verandas overlooking the Saadani National Park. This has to be the best way to combine luxury safari with a relaxing beach getaway.

Uganda

Sanctuary Gorilla Forest Camp

This camp is tucked away deep inside Bwindi Impenetrable Forest, a UNESCO World Heritage Site in southwest Uganda, and home to just over half the world's last surviving mountain gorillas. Seeing these gentle giants within their natural habitat is a unique opportunity afforded to a select few, as just eight visitors are allowed to view each habituated group each day. Sanctuary Gorilla Forest Camp is the perfect luxurious base for a gorilla tracking experience.

Kenya

Sanctuary Olonana Safari Camp

Sanctuary Olonana is located in the Masai Mara, the heart of Kenya's big-game country. Fourteen spacious en-suite tents border the banks of the Mara River, where the resident hippo spend their days wallowing. A wide range of game and cultural activities are available, including the great wildebeest migration from around July to October each year. The camp earned a gold award from Ecotourism Kenya for its innovative wetlands and tree planting projects.

Sanctuary Private Camping

Sanctuary Private Camping is the ultimate and most authentic form of safari. Private tented camps are set up in hand-picked wildlife areas in Kenya and Tanzania, to create an experience to suit guests' individual tastes. Tents are large, with en-suite bathrooms and each tent has a personal attendant. This unique type of safari camp allows for a cherished bush experience, without leaving a lasting footprint on the environment.

Recipe index

Page numbers in *italic* indicate photos.